D0300890

GOLD MEDAL GUIDE

the [illegible] r

[illegible] ..rst

# GOLDFISH

AMANDA O'NEILL

Interpet Publishing

**Editor:** Philip de Ste. Croix
**Designer:** Philip Clucas MSIAD
**Studio photography:**
Neil Sutherland
**Specialist advice:** Nick Fletcher
**Production management:**
Consortium, Poslingford, Suffolk

Published by Interpet Publishing,
Vincent Lane, Dorking,
Surrey RH4 3YX, England

© 2004 Interpet Publishing Ltd.
All rights reserved

ISBN 1-84286-091-7

**Print production:**
Sino Publishing House Ltd., Hong Kong
**Printed and bound** in the Far East

**The Author** Amanda O'Neill was born in Sussex in 1951 and educated at the University of Exeter, where she read medieval literature. She has never lived without a variety of pets, ranging from rabbits and gerbils to giant snails and hissing cockroaches. Currently she lives in the Midlands with her husband and son, along with five dogs, a cat, Roborowski hamsters and a collection of coldwater fish.

*The recommendations in this book are given without any guarantees o the part of the author and publishe If in doubt, seek the advice of a ve or pet-care specialist.*

# Contents

ACC. No. 578778
PRICE
CLASS 639.374 LIB C

# INTRODUCTION

## 1 Goldfish are the most popular household pets in the world

Goldfish are the hardiest of aquarium fish. After the initial cost of setting up their home, they are cheap and easy to care for. In fact, they make the ideal pet for people who lack the time or space for a more demanding creature, but beyond that they have advantages in their own right. The common goldfish is an uncommonly beautiful creature, with its brilliant colouring and graceful movements. Fish in a well-maintained aquarium are a joy to watch, and provide a great antidote to the stress of modern life.

*Above: Aquarium furnishings can be as simple or elaborate as you like. Rocks and plants provide an attractive setting, and also make life more interesting for the fish.*

## 2 Goldfish are living ornaments

They form a decorative feature in any room. Unlike other ornaments, however, they require a degree of commitment in terms of time and attention. Compared with most ets, goldfish are very low-maintenance – they can even e left for up to a week when you go on holiday. lonetheless they will not survive real neglect. The artificial nvironment in which they live needs to be set up with are in the first place, and then needs regular cleaning and vater changes to keep the water healthy and allow the fish ) breathe.

## 3 Goldfish have a long history as pets

ney originated more than a iousand years ago in southern China, where sh breeders discovered that the drab-coloured vild Crucian Carp, normally a dull brass colour, occasionally roduced 'sports' with brighter colours, shinier scales or nusual fin shapes. Selective breeding from these natural iutations developed various ornamental forms with the naracteristic golden colour. Later, Japanese and Korean sh breeders contributed their expertise to the development f further varieties. The goldfish reached Europe in the xteenth century nd the USA in the neteenth century, oing on to spread cross the world.

*Right: Goldfish can ırvive in an unfurnished tank, but they will be happier, healthier and easier to care for in a well-designed environment like this.*

### GOLD MEDAL TIPS

**A LONG LIFESPAN**

*Goldfish are long-lived. Given the right living conditions, they may attain 25 years or more – the record is 43 years, but this is unusual. In ponds and large aquariums, they may live 15 to 20 years. In smaller aquariums, a 5-10 year lifespan is more likely.*

**ANCESTRAL COLOURS**

*Goldfish are not gold when they first hatch, but a drab greenish brown colour harking back to their wild ancestors. Most then go through a black or dark brown stage before turning golden. However, some individuals inherit their ancestors'. colour and will remain brown or bronze.*

**COUSIN KOI**

*The Japanese koi resembles the goldfish in many respects, but is descended from a different species of carp and has two pairs of 'whiskers' (barbels) around the mouth. Do not confuse the two! Koi are not suited to aquariums, as they grow to a much greater size (up to a metre long) and require a large, deep pool.*

# GOLD MEDAL TIPS

**_DON'T TOUCH!_**

*Fish scales are covered by a thin layer of skin, which produces lubricating mucus to help the fish to glide through the water and also to guard against infection. If you need to handle your goldfish, make sure you have wet hands to avoid damaging this fragile skin.*

*Below: The mouth acts rather like a vacuum cleaner nozzle.*

**_SPECIAL JAWS_**

*Goldfish have protrusible mouthparts, and food is 'sucked' in by a partial vacuum created by the action of their gills. Their mouths are toothless, but they have special teeth located well back in their throats to grind up food as it goes down.*

**_BEDTIME_**

*Yes, goldfish do sleep at night, although they cannot close their eyes. Sleeping goldfish usually sink to the bottom of the tank and their colours fade slightly. They sleep best in the dark, so turn off tank lights at night. They need undisturbed sleep to remain healthy.*

# KNOW YOUR

## 4 Why goldfish are gold

The goldfish's scales are actually transparent. Beneath them lies a thin layer of skin containing pigment (colour) cells and also a layer of crystalline material called guanine. It is the guanine which creates the characteristic metallic sheen. Not all goldfish are metallic: some varieties lack guanine, and they have a 'matt' rather than 'gloss' appearance. The actual colour of the fish (for not all goldfish are golden) depends on the type and combination of pigment cells, and indeed there are white (silver) goldfish which have no pigment cells at all.

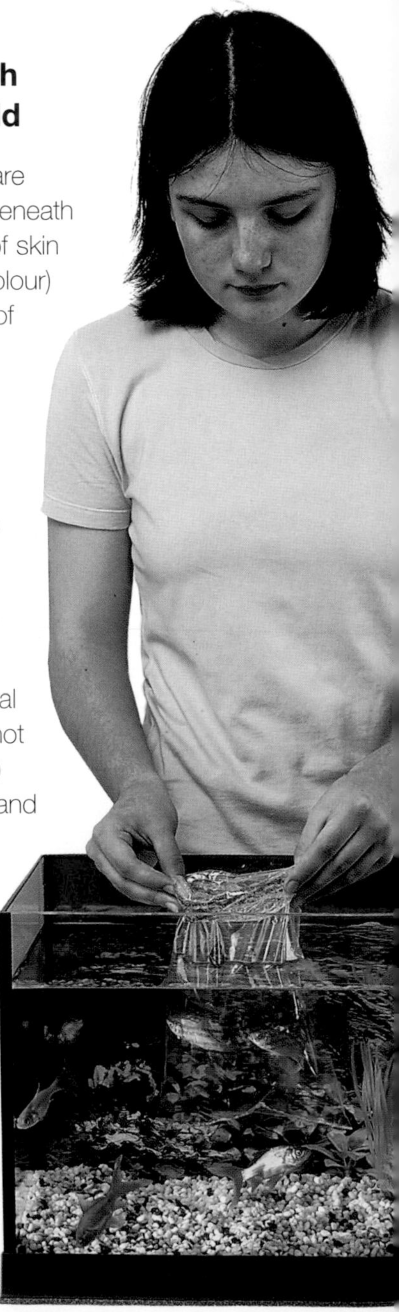

*Right: Fish have a highly efficient respiratory system, but they need clean, well-aerated water to supply enough oxygen to breathe.*

# GOLDFISH

5

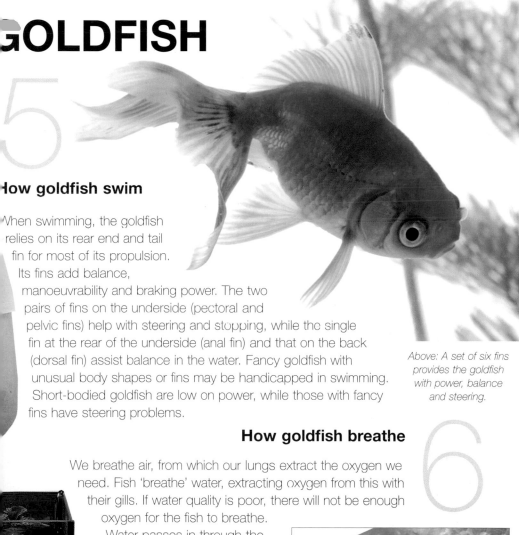

## How goldfish swim

When swimming, the goldfish relies on its rear end and tail fin for most of its propulsion. Its fins add balance, manoeuvrability and braking power. The two pairs of fins on the underside (pectoral and pelvic fins) help with steering and stopping, while the single fin at the rear of the underside (anal fin) and that on the back (dorsal fin) assist balance in the water. Fancy goldfish with unusual body shapes or fins may be handicapped in swimming. Short-bodied goldfish are low on power, while those with fancy fins have steering problems.

*Above: A set of six fins provides the goldfish with power, balance and steering.*

## How goldfish breathe

6

We breathe air, from which our lungs extract the oxygen we need. Fish 'breathe' water, extracting oxygen from this with their gills. If water quality is poor, there will not be enough oxygen for the fish to breathe. Water passes in through the fish's mouth and out through the gills, inside which thread-like blood vessels near the surface take in oxygen and pass out waste carbon dioxide. The gills are covered by a protective shield called the operculum, whose curved shape you can clearly see behind the eye.

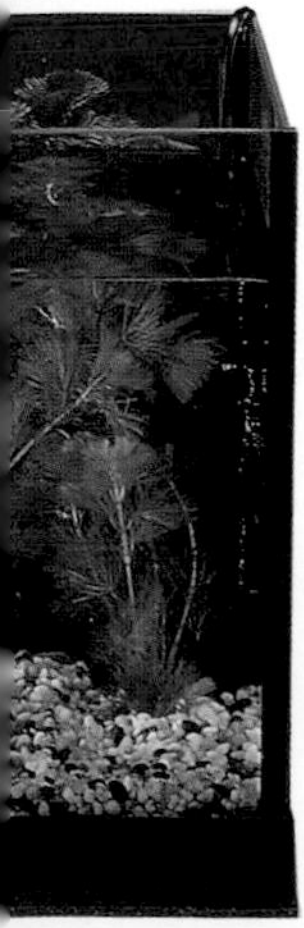

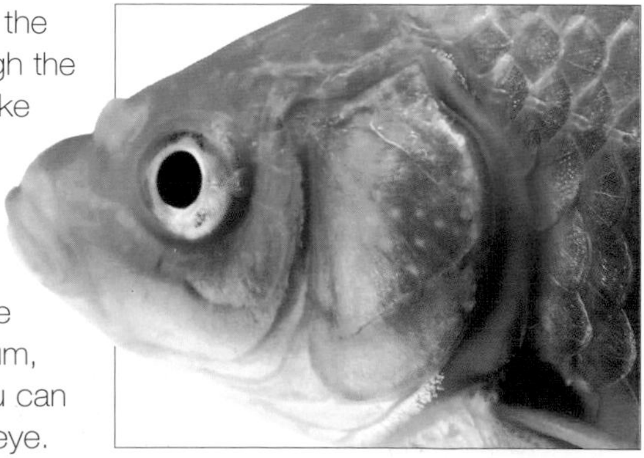

# EASY VARIETIES

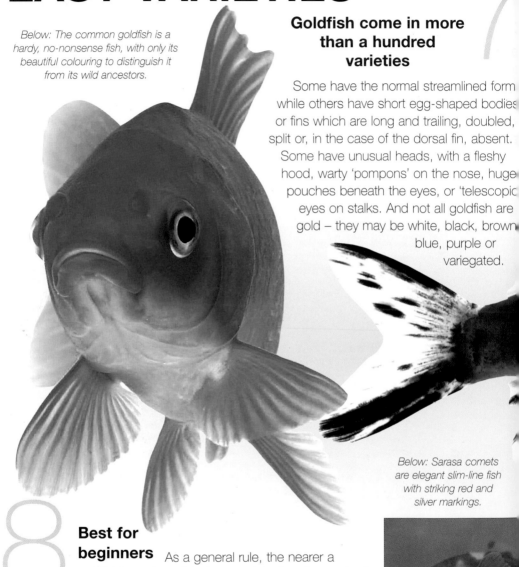

*Below: The common goldfish is a hardy, no-nonsense fish, with only its beautiful colouring to distinguish it from its wild ancestors.*

## 7 Goldfish come in more than a hundred varieties

Some have the normal streamlined form while others have short egg-shaped bodies or fins which are long and trailing, doubled, split or, in the case of the dorsal fin, absent. Some have unusual heads, with a fleshy hood, warty 'pompons' on the nose, huge pouches beneath the eyes, or 'telescopic' eyes on stalks. And not all goldfish are gold – they may be white, black, brown, blue, purple or variegated.

*Below: Sarasa comets are elegant slim-line fish with striking red and silver markings.*

**8 Best for beginners** As a general rule, the nearer a goldfish is to the original, natural design, the easier it is to keep. The common goldfish, which resembles its wild ancestor in all but colour, is the hardiest of the tribe. With no exaggeration to distract the eye from its beautiful colour and metallic sheen, it is also one of the most attractive. It is the most popular goldfish, and is recommended for novice fishkeepers.

## Shubunkins are also suitable for the novice

9

ne shubunkin is a very distinctive colour ariety combining matt and metallic scales. is shaped like the common goldfish, but eautifully patterned, with a silvery blue background peckled with black spots and patched with areas of olet, red, orange, yellow or brown. It was developed in apan, and its name means 'brocade' (a patterned fabric).

Shubunkins come in two main varieties, the London (normal finnage) and the Bristol (longer, rounded fins, especially the tail).

*Below: A richly patterned shubunkin.*

## Comets are easy to keep, but need more space

10

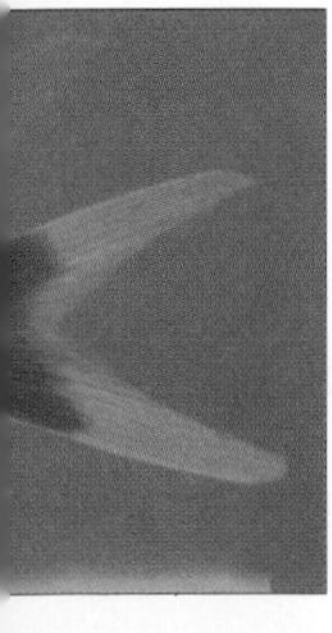

The comet is a 'stretch' version of the common goldfish, with slimmer body and longer fins, especially the deeply forked tail fin, which may be as long as the fish's body. It comes in all the metallic colours, including variegated, and also in non-metallic calico (black mottling and coloured patches on a silvery blue background).

## GOLD MEDAL TIPS

### Varying sizes

*Given good conditions and plenty of space, common goldfish and also London shubunkins can reach 20cm (8in) or more. Comets do not attain the same size (though they can grow quite large, given the space), while Bristol shubunkins remain small, rarely exceeding 12cm (5in).*

### Japanese edition

*The wakin is Japan's version of the common goldfish. Very similar in appearance apart from its double, fan-like tail fin and slightly deeper body, it is another hardy variety. However, it needs a larger tank, as it can grow considerably larger than its common cousin, reaching 30cm (12in) in length.*

*Above: A common goldfish.*

### Special comets

*Variegated red and silver comets are particularly popular, especially the sarasa, with a silver base and red markings throughout the body. Less common but equally striking is the tancho, which is entirely silver apart from a circular red 'cap' on the head.*

# FANCY VARIETIES

## 11 Fancy goldfish are usually more delicate

The more a variety departs from the 'natural' goldfish shape, the more likely it is to need extra care. There are three main areas which novices should approach with caution: body shape, fin shape and eyes. Egg-shaped goldfish with short fat bodies are more fragile, long trailing fins require more care than the shorter type, and bulging eyes are prone to injury and infection.

*Red and black globe-eye*

*Beautiful or grotesque? The development of fancy goldfish has taken them far beyond the simple shapes of their wild ancestors. Exaggerated features mean that they may require extra care.*

*Calico ryukin*

*Oranda*

## 12 Egg-shaped goldfish

Short-bodied (egg-shaped) varieties such as the fantail and oranda have a shorter swimbladder, the organ which provides buoyancy and enables a fish to maintain its balance. This makes them slower, more awkward swimmers and also more prone to swimbladder disease, which affects ability to swim – affected fish may sink to the bottom of the tank or float helplessly on top. The compression of the body may also affect digestion, so special attention needs to be paid to their diet.

13

## Fancy fins

Long, trailing, double fins are graceful and attractive. They are also at greater risk than normal fins of injury, infection and parasite infestation. Long-finned fish are slower swimmers than 'normal' goldfish and more sensitive to water temperature. Fantails and Japanese ryukin, with fins of moderate length, are reasonably easy to maintain, but veiltails are not recommended for the novice.

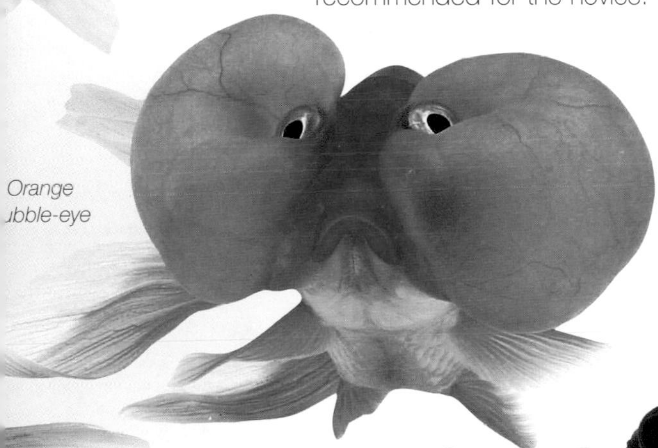

Orange bubble-eye

14

## Goggle eyes

A number of varieties have abnormal eye configurations. The 'globe-eye' is commonest, with bulbous protruding eyes. These globe eyes take two to three years to develop fully. Even more extreme are celestial goldfish, with hugely protruding eyes permanently turned upwards, and bubble-eyes, with vast fluid-filled balloons around their eyes. Goggle-eyed fish tend to be delicate. They have difficulty seeing and finding food, and are prone to eye injury and infection.

## GOLD MEDAL TIPS

**DON'T MIX!**

*Comets, shubunkins and common goldfish are tougher, faster, more active and more aggressive than fancier varieties. Don't try to house the two types together, or the latter may become stressed or injured, and will find it hard to compete for their share of food.*

**HOODED ORANDA**

*The egg-shaped oranda is a popular aquarium fish. It is characterized by a warty growth on the head which grows to form a 'hood' – particularly notable in the red cap oranda, a silver fish with a red hood. However, this fish is vulnerable to swimbladder disease and fungal infections.*

*Moor*

**MOORS**

*The moor is another striking variety, with an egg-shaped body, trailing fins, protruding eyes and dramatic black colouring. Although popular, it is not one for the novice. Its vulnerable eyes and fins need particular care, and it is more sensitive to water temperature than tougher varieties.*

# THE AQUARIUM

15

## Choose your container with care

Traditional goldfish bowls are not recommended, as they offer only a small water surface area to absorb oxygen. However, it is now possible to buy a large-capacity 'all-in-one' goldfish bowl with built-in air pump and filtration system, which provides the right environment for fish. The alternative is a glass or plastic aquarium. These are available in various shapes and sizes, but a long rectangular tank is usually better than a tall, narrow one – surface area for oxygenation is more important than depth of water. Some tanks available in pet shops are more ornamental than practical.

16

## What size?

Buy the biggest tank you can accommodate, to provide optimal living conditions for your fish. The smaller the container, the less oxygen is available for the fish, and the faster the water becomes polluted with goldfish waste. Goldfish are active and also fast-growing, so they appreciate space. If you have room, a 55-litre (12gal) tank 60cm (24in) long, 30cm (12in) wide and 30cm (12in) deep is a good start. This would house five young goldfish quite comfortably and allow them room to grow.

*Right: Although quite small, these linked plastic tanks, with an air stone in each section, provide more space than a conventional goldfish bowl.*

17

## Choosing the right site for your aquarium is important

You want to enjoy easy viewing, and the fish want to enjoy peace and quiet without the risk of passers-by bumping into their home. The ideal site will be also be well away from draughts or heat sources, to avoid sudden or extreme changes of temperature, and not in direct sunlight, which will over-heat the water, reduce its oxygen content and encourage the growth of algae. You also want an electrical socket nearby, so that you can plug in a filter, light and other equipment without having hazardous railing wires.

ove: This odern globe s a built-in pump and ation system.

ght: The rtical design ovides less ater surface ea for ygenation an a horizontal ne, so a pump essential to rate the water fectively.

## GOLD MEDAL TIPS

**GLASS OR PLASTIC?**

*Plastic tanks are less durable and tend to be available only in smaller sizes. Modern all-glass tanks are strong and easily cleaned. Metal-framed glass tanks are rarely seen nowadays: if you do have one, seal the joints with silicone before use and seek advice on cleaning.*

**WEIGHTY MATTERS**

*Once filled with water, an aquarium is surprisingly heavy. A 40-litre (9gal) tank fully set up weighs about 90kg (200lb)! Make sure your tank is set on a base strong enough to take the weight. The base must also be completely level to prevent stress to the glass. Cushion it with a thick sheet of polystyrene.*

*Above: Check that the aquarium is secure and level before filling.*

**COVERS**

*A secure and ventilated aquarium cover is strongly recommended as a safety precaution against both suicidal fish leaping out and hungry cats prying in. It also reduces water loss by evaporation. Many aquarium covers now incorporate a light to illuminate the tank.*

# GOLD MEDAL TIPS

**_FILTER MAINTENANCE_**

*Mechanical filter media need regular cleaning to remain effective. How often you need to do this depends on your aquarium set-up (for example, how many fish you have). Don't wash filters under the tap, as tap water may destroy beneficial bacteria: use water from the aquarium itself.*

**_LIGHTING_**

*Lighting is an attractive extra and also encourages plant growth. Fluorescent lighting is recommended – ordinary light bulbs are unsuitable, as they heat up the water. Lamp fittings must be shielded from condensation and splashes by protective glass. Most modern aquariums come complete with suitable light hoods.*

**_HEATING_**

*Goldfish are coldwater fish. They don't need a heater in their tank unless you live somewhere where winters are very cold and the temperature of the tank drops below 18°C/65°F. They are more likely to need a fan to cool the water surface during the hot summer months.*

# ELECTRICA

## 18 Installing a pump and filter is well worthwhile

Maintaining good water quality is the key to goldfish survival. Water is a fish's life support from which i obtains oxygen to breathe – but also a fish's toilet. In the small, closed environment of an aquarium, oxygen is quickly used up, and waste products build up to poison the fish. Regular partial water changes (see p. 24) go a long way towards improving aeration and removing waste but a pump and filter make this task easier and keep oxygen levels high.

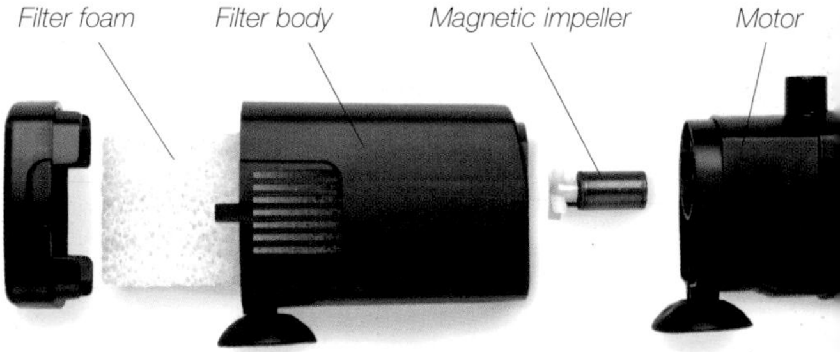


*Above: An underwater filter dismantled to show its component parts.*

## 19 A filter cleans the water by removing waste

It draws the water through a filtering medium and traps solid particles, returning clean water to the tank. Biological filter also develop beneficial bacteria which break down waste products produced by the fish and render them harmless There are many different kinds of filter available, including box filters and undergravel filters, powered by an air pump and internal and external power filters, which have their own pumps. Your local aquatic shop will be able to advis you on what best suits your aquarium.

# :QUIPMENT

## 20

## An air pump increases the amount of oxygen in the water

Rising bubbles from the airstone oxygenate the water.

ıe pump is attached to an airstone ıich pushes out a stream of bubbles, ·culating and aerating the water, and so helping waste gases (carbon oxide and ammonia) to pass out of e water through the surface. Most ımps need to be positioned on a ıelf above the level of the tank, to event water siphoning backwards. ıe same pump can operate both a ox or undergravel filter and an air ıpply to the airstone. Seek advice on e best type for your tank.

## 21

## afety first

'ater and ectricity make dangerous combination. When etting up a tank with a pump, filter or hting, make sure all wires are tucked ıfely out of the way where no one will o over them, and invest in a circuit eaker to cut off the power if there is ı accident. Treat electrical equipment ith respect. Always switch off the ower before handling it, and never uch either the equipment or switches ith wet hands.

# AQUASCAPING

22

## Aquarium furnishings

Decorating your aquarium wit plants, rocks and ornaments creates a pleasing effect to th human eye and also makes a more interesting environment for fish. Goldfish prefer a world with a few places to hide rather than a totally bare environment. It is up to you whether you choos a natural look or create a fantasy underwater kingdom. A printed backdrop stuck to the back of the tank will continue your theme while concealing wires etc. in the background.

*Above: A printed backdrop provides the finishing touch to your aquarium décor, as well as hiding unsightly wires and other visual distractions.*

23

## Aquatic plants add to the beauty of your aquarium

They also help aerate the water and provide your fish with shelter and nutritious nibbles. Choose plants suitable for coldwater aquariums. Goldfish do enjoy eating plants, and also tend to uproot them from the gravel when feeding, so you may need to replace plants from time to time. Plants rooted in rock wool are more secure than bare-rooted ones. Alternatively you can buy plastic plants, which last forever and only need cleaning to maintain their appearance.

*Plastic plants and professionally treated driftwood are safe decorations for your tank.*

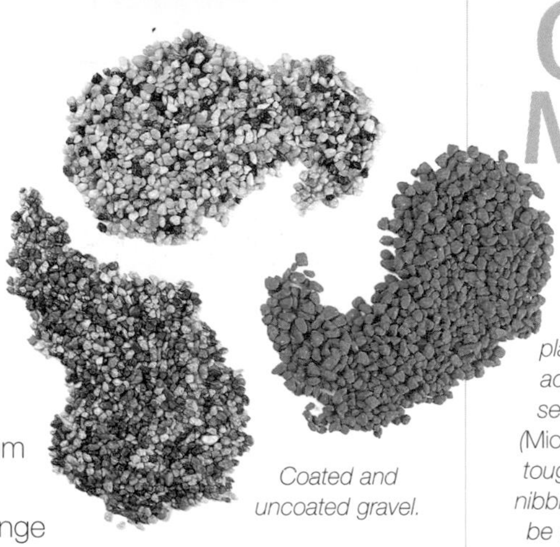

Coated and uncoated gravel.

## 24

## The aquarium floor

ravel or sand is usually sed to cover the aquarium oor. Aquatic dealers and etshops stock a wide range f gravels, both natural and coloured and in different sizes, hich are safe for aquarium use. Medium-sized gravel is est – fine gravel or sand cannot be used with undergravel ters, and coarser gravel may lodge in a fish's throat. Do not e tempted to collect your own gravel or sand from versides or beaches – it may be polluted.

## 25

## Rocks and ornaments

Aquatic dealers and petshops are also the safest source of rocks and ornaments, ensuring avoidance of rocks with sharp edges, which might injure your fish, and calcium-based rocks, whose mineral content affects the water chemistry. A wide variety of ornaments is available, including figures powered by the airpump. Don't be tempted by ornaments not designed for aquariums, as some plastics and metals are toxic to fish.

## GOLD MEDAL TIPS

**TOUGH LEAVES**

*Your local aquatic dealer should have a selection of plants suitable for a coldwater aquarium. One that is worth seeking out is the Java fern* (Microsorium pteropus)*, whose tough leaves are proof against nibbling. Soft-leaved plants may be too appetizing to last long!*

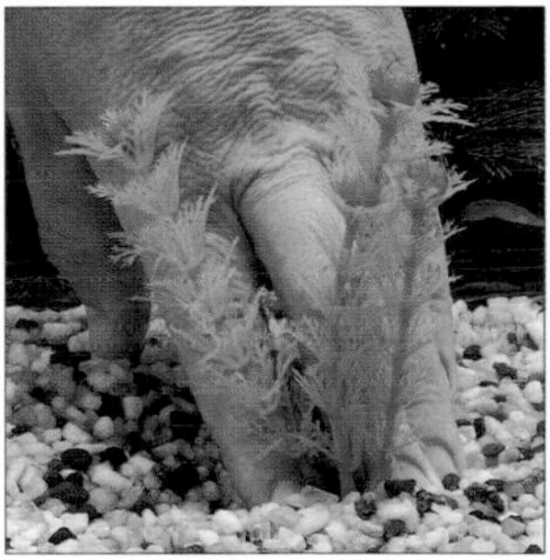

*Above: Plants need rooting securely into the gravel.*

**AVOID SEASHELLS**

*Seashells and coral may look like suitable decorations for an aquarium, but don't risk using them. They may leach out chemicals into the water, making it too alkaline for goldfish. They also create a hygiene problem, as they tend to trap waste particles.*

**DRIFTWOOD DÉCOR**

*Pieces of driftwood used as tank ornaments are another potential hazard. Never use pieces picked up from a beach. Driftwood needs expert cleaning and curing to make it safe, so only pieces labelled as fit for this purpose are suitable.*

GOLD MEDAL TIPS

**TAP WATER**

*Goldfish are remarkably tolerant as regards water. You can buy test kits to check the pH level or the hardness or softness of your local tap water, but your fish should be able to cope with it anyway. Just remember to dechlorinate your water as described in Tip 27.*

**TANK CYCLING**

*If you suddenly add fish to a new tank, their waste will build up ammonia in the water before beneficial bacteria develop in the filter to tackle this, and the fish will be poisoned. Protect your fish by maturing water beforehand and not adding too many fish at once.*

*Above: Rinse gravel thoroughly before use, stirring it hard until the water runs clear.*

**GRATEFUL FOR GRAVEL**

*Most fishkeepers feel that gravel makes an attractive aquarium flooring. Goldfish are natural bottom-feeders and enjoy rooting around in it, and it provides a growing medium for plants. It is always sensible and humane to provide some gravel as a substrate for your fish.*

# PREPARING THE AQUARIUM

26

## Plan your lay-out before adding water

Start with the gravel (unless you have an undergravel filter, which needs to be put in first), rinsing it thoroughly before use. Lay the gravel deeper at the back of the tank, sloping towards the front. This makes cleaning easier by encouraging debris to drift to the front, where it can be siphoned off. Position rocks and ornaments, pushing their bases securely into the gravel. Now place your pump and airstone in place and tuck the airline under the gravel. You can use a rock to conceal the airstone.

*Below: Pouring water on to a plate avoids disturbing the gravel. Far right: A chemical dechlorinator wi[ll] ensure that th[e] water is saf[e] for fish.*

*Above: Special tools are available to help planting.*

27

## Now add water

When you are satisfied with your arrangement, you can start adding the water – ordinary tap water will do provided that you treat it with a conditioner to remove harmful chlorine disinfectants. To avoid dislodging the gravel and spoiling your careful lay-out, lay a small plate on top of the gravel and pour the water slowly on to this. When the aquarium is half-full, add the plants, tucking roots under the gravel and weighting them down with small rocks. Now you can add the rest of the water. If you have a power filter, this should be the last item you install.

## Be patient when setting up your aquarium

28

Now comes the difficult part: do nothing! Start the filter running, then leave the aquarium alone for at least three days before you bring your fish home. (Even if you don't have a filter, remember to add a chemical dechlorinator, available from any petshop.) This rest period allows the water to mature, dissipating any chlorine and establishing the temperature. Allowing the water to mature in this way ensures a safe environment for your new fish and gives plants time to establish themselves.

GOLD MEDAL TIPS

**START SMALL**

*Small, young fish may not look very impressive compared with full-grown specimens, but they are the best purchase as they will settle in better. They will soon grow, and you will have the pleasure of watching them develop under your care into handsome specimens.*

**DON'T MIX**

*Don't be tempted to mix small goldfish with large ones. The larger fish will tend to grab all the food, leaving their smaller tank-mates hungry. The same applies if you mix fast swimmers like comets or shubunkins with slow swimmers like veiltails – the latter will lose out.*

**WATER SNAILS**

*Some people like to include water snails in their tank, but these can cause problems. They may eat up some waste matter, but they produce more themselves. They also devour aquarium plants – and often breed so successfully that you may be overrun with snails.*

# 29

## Buy fish from a reputable source

Good aquatic dealers, petshops and private breeders will have well-kept fish and knowledgeable staff. Check the aquariums: cloudy water, over-crowding or dead fish lying on the bottom mean you should go elsewhere. Then look at the fish themselves. They should be active and free-moving, not skulking, floating or gulping for air at the surface. Avoid any fish with spots, sores, lumps, parasites or damaged fins – and their tank-mates, as such problems may be contagious. Ask staff about goldfish care: if they don't know the answers, fish in their care are unlikely to thrive.

*Left: Choose your fish carefully. A healthy goldfish should swim freely and without effort, although long-finned fancy varieties will move more slowly.*

# YOUR FIRST FISH

30

## How many fish can your tank accommodate?

alculate the surface area of your tank. The general rule is 1cm f fish per 60sq cm (1in per 24sq in) of water surface area. So tank measuring 60cm x 30cm x 30cm has a surface area of 1800sq cm which means it an hold a total of 30cm of fish. And remember that your fish will grow, so allow for this. If ou do not have a pump and filter, go for the minimum number of fish. In any case, it is ways better to under-stock than over-stock, to give your fish the best possible living onditions. Ideally, buy one or two small fish to start with and wait a w weeks before adding more. This allows e tank to mature, gradually eveloping beneficial acteria in the filter to ckle waste.

*Above: Check fins for any damage, which may indicate infection.*

31

## Bringing your fish home

Your fish will be supplied in a plastic bag of water. Don't just tip them straight into your aquarium. Float the unopened bag in the tank for about 20 minutes so that the water temperature can equalize. The water in the transit bag will be polluted with fish waste so you do not want it to mix with the tank water. After ten minutes, open the bag and gently lift the fish into the tank with wet hands. Discard the transit water. The fish need to be left in peace to settle in, so wait till next morning to start feeding.

# FOOD AND FEEDING

## 32 What should I feed my goldfish?

*Above: Frozen bloodworms (left) and mosquito larvae (right) need to be thawed out before serving them as food to your fish.*

Commercially produced goldfish food, in flake or pellet form, should provide the mainstay of the diet. Most goldfish keepers favour flakes, which float well and are easily nibbled. In addition, to ensure that all the fish's nutritional needs are met, provide occasional treats of small quantities of finely shredded greens (lettuce, spinach, shelled peas, etc.) and live food. Suitable live foods include daphnia (water fleas), brine shrimps and bloodworms, bought live from pet-stores. Don't try catching your own from a local pond as they may introduce disease. These foods are also available in frozen form.

## 33 How much?

enerally, give only as
uch as your fish will
at in five minutes.
or the first few
ays, give a small
mount and time the
sh eating. If they
nish early, offer a little
ore, and if they are still
ating when the time is
p, feed less next time, until
ou have the amount right.
oldfish are greedy: given the chance, they will eat
ntil they are too full to swim. Over-feeding is
ore dangerous than under-feeding. Over-fed
goldfish produce more waste than
filters can handle, while left-over
food fouls the water further.

## 34 How often?

Above: Fish pellets and flakes.

Young, growing fish need extra rations, so they should be fed twice or even three times a day. As they grow, this can be cut down to once a day. Fully mature goldfish can
e fed once every other day. If you feed too often, your
oldfish will become fat and unhealthy. Healthy goldfish will
urvive for a week or more without food. If you are going
n holiday for a week, your fish will probably be safer left
nfed than trusted to a friend who may over-feed them.

## GOLD MEDAL TIPS

### SPECIAL FOODS

*Only buy fish food made specifically for goldfish, as not all species of fish have the same nutritional feeds. Look for foods which are labelled as providing complete balanced nutrition. The right diet will not only keep your fish healthy but help to develop their colour to its full potential.*

### LITTLE AND OFTEN

*In the wild, goldfish 'graze', eating small amounts continuously. This is the ideal regime for their very simple digestive systems to handle. So, if you are at home all day, breaking up the daily feed into three or four mini-meals a day will suit them very well. It also makes their life more varied and interesting.*

### DELICATE DIGESTION

*Short-bodied ('egg-shaped') fish may need extra care with feeding. They are prone to buoyancy problems (see page 10), and floating foods can cause a problem if the fish gulp air when feeding. It pays to soak their food for a minute or so beforehand so that it sinks below the surface.*

GOLD MEDAL TIPS

**SAFETY FIRST**

*When cleaning your tank, remember to switch off all electrical equipment and unplug it at the mains before you start work, to protect yourself (and your fish). Take care not to splash nearby electrical sockets. Remember, water and electricity don't mix!*

**NO SOAP PLEASE**

*Never clean the tank or any ornaments with soap or household cleaning products, which might poison your fish. Don't even risk cleaning the outside glass with products designed for windows: stick to cleaners specially designed for aquarium use, stocked by petshops and aquatic centres.*

**GRAVEL CARE**

*Debris accumulates in the gravel on the tank floor. Visible debris can be vacuumed up either when you notice it or during the weekly cleaning routine. In addition, it helps to stir the top layer gently every two weeks to allow water to circulate through it.*

# AQUARIUM MAINTENANCE

## 35 Useful cleaning kit

Your basic cleaning kit should consist of a siphoning vacuum for cleaning the tank and changing water, an algae scrubber, and a pair of buckets, one for removing old water from the tank and the other for maturing replacement water. Reserve these buckets for aquarium use only. Choose a siphon with an attachment for vacuuming the gravel, to remove fish waste, left-over food and other organic material. These tasks are essential: a neglected environment means dead fish!

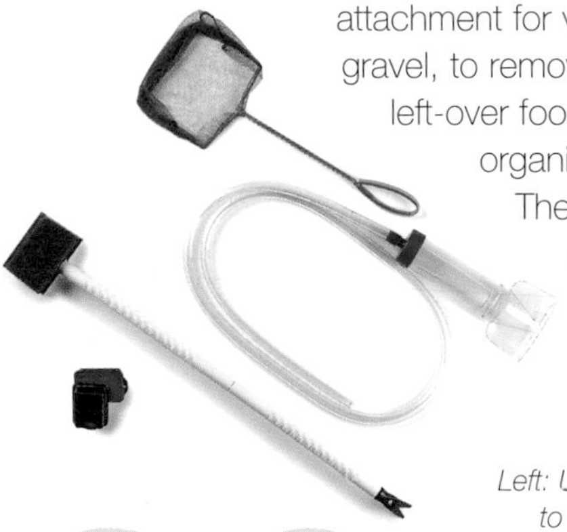

*Left: Useful tools include a net to catch fish, a vacuum siphon and an algae scrubber.*

## 36 Filtration removes considerable pollution, but not all

So, once a week (more often if you don't have a filter), siphon out a third of the tank water and replace it with fresh. Don't use water straight from the tap – fill a bucket the day before and let it stand overnight to reach room temperature and use a water conditioner to remove any chlorine. This task must be carried out regularly to avoid sudden changes to water chemistry, which are as dangerous to the fish as neglecting the water.

## 37 Filter maintenance

Pumps and filters also need regular attention. Check the instructions for your particular models, but in general filter media need replacing periodically and filter elements should be rinsed out weekly. Be sure to rinse in used tank water, not under the tap – tap water destroys beneficial bacteria. Check that the airstone is not clogged with algae or chemical deposits and that the air hose is free of kinks. These checks can be carried out at the same time as the weekly water change.

## 38 Remove any algae

Once your tank is matured, algae are likely to start growing. If there is only a little, it is harmless, and in fact the fish will enjoy nibbling at it. Algae are easily removed from glass with an algae scrubber as part of your weekly routine. Too much light stimulates algae growth, so if dense algae obscures the glass, turns the water green or smothers plants, move your aquarium to a shadier spot to help solve the problem.

*Left: An algae scrubber has an abrasive surface to remove algae from the glass before it grows thick enough to cause a problem.*

# UNDERSTANDING YOUF

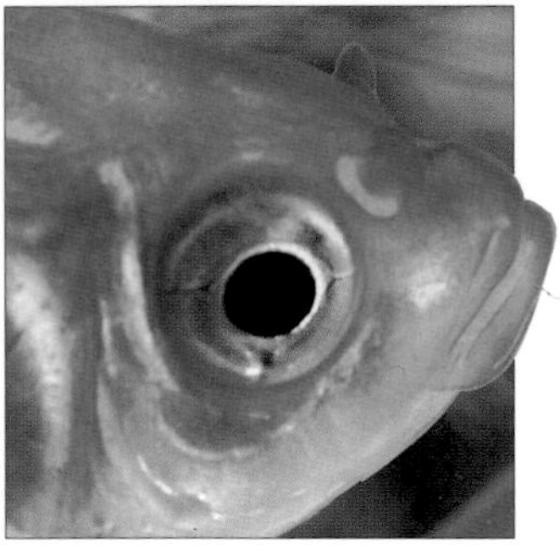

Above: Each eye can focus independently, giving the goldfish a panoramic field of vision.

## 39 Goldfish have good eyesight, up to a point

They are short-sighted, but see nearby objects well, and have colour vision. Eyes positioned on the sides of their heads giv them a wider field of view than ours. Unlike ours, their eyes cannot cope with sudden changes in light intensity, because they lack eyelids and also irises (the part of the eye which changes size to admit varying amounts of light), so they appreciate plants and other cover where they can shelter when lights are switched on or off.

## 40 Goldfish don't have ears – but they can hear

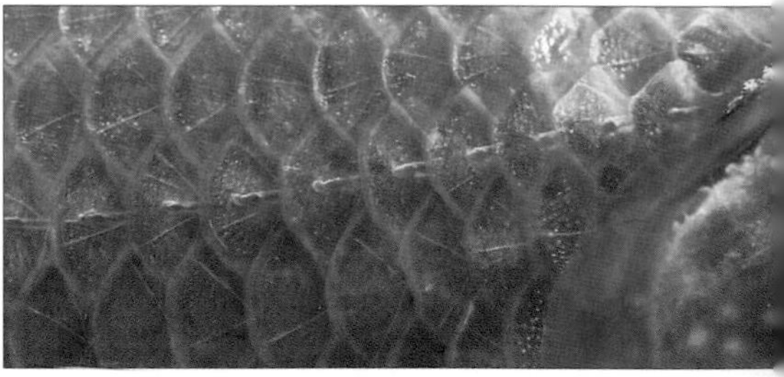

Above: The sensory lateral line is clearly visible running along the sides of the goldfish's body.

They have an organ inside the head, similar to our inner ear, which detects sound vibrations. In addition they have a row of nerve cells running down their sides (visible as a fine horizontal line), called the lateral line, which picks up sound and othe vibrations. These two 'alternative ears' enable goldfish to hear sounds inside and outside their aquarium. The lateral line also detect pressure changes in the water, allowing th fish to sense and avoi any obstacles.

Left: Sound travels through water more than four times faster than it does through air, so fish respond quickly to sound vibrations.

# GOLDFISH

41

## They don't have noses, but they can smell

A fish's nostrils, one on either side of the snout, are not used for reathing and do not connect with the mouth or throat. heir purpose is simply to smell. Water passes in and out rough the nostrils, where sensory cells register the cents it carries. Although a goldfish's sense of smell is ot very keen, it is quite important for finding food. In dirty ater, the fish cannot smell their food and may have ifficulty in locating it.

## Goldfish are sociable creatures

42

hey are generally peaceable nd tend to seek each other's ompany. Aggression is only kely to occur during the breeding season, or if a tank-ate is injured, when others may pick on it. However, oldfish do not appear to suffer if kept alone. If space is mited, a single fish will be happier living alone with room o move than several fish crammed into a small area.

## GOLD MEDAL TIPS

**INTELLIGENCE**

*It has long been known that goldfish can learn to recognize their owners – and their feeding times. Recent research which established that they can learn to identify different tunes suggests that they may be much brighter than we used to think.*

*Above: Taste sensors inside the mouth identify edible objects.*

**A MATTER OF TASTE**

*Goldfish have a good sense of taste. They have plenty of taste buds, located in the lips and all over the mouth. They use their mouths to explore their surroundings for food, quickly identifying what is edible and spitting out anything that is not.*

**SOUND SENSITIVITY**

*Don't bang on the glass! Glass walls and water insulate your fish from normal sounds outside the aquarium such as conversation. However, if you tap on the glass or even the table under the tank, they will register this as a very loud noise indeed and may become quite distressed.*

# COMMON AILMENTS

43

## Prevention is better than cure

The commonest cause of illness in goldfish is poor water quality, so don't neglect water changes, maintain filtration and aeration systems in good order, and avoid over-feeding and over-crowding. Introducing new fish, plants or tank ornaments can bring in diseases, so don't add anything to the aquarium unless it comes from a safe source (a reputable aquatic dealer or petshop). If you have space for a second tank, quarantine any new fish in this for a month before introduction.

*Fin rot is a bacterial disease that erodes the living tissue, leaving the bony rays protruding.*

*Whitespot is a parasitic infection characterized by the presence of white pimples.*

*Areas of redness or ulcers are caused by bacterial infection.*

*In fish affected by dropsy, the scales protrude from the body surface, rather like a pine cone.*

44

## Warning signs

Changes in a fish's behaviour or appearance should never be ignored. A fish which is more active or less active than usual, or reluctant to feed, may be ill. Sick fish may float, sink, whirl or swim sideways. Other signs to beware include sudden bloating, fins clamped tightly to the body, fish scratching themselves against tank objects, sticky faeces trailing from the vent, and spots, sores or discoloration of the skin. Seek advice on treatment from your aquatic dealer.

## 45 Spots and rots

Damage or blemishes to a fish's skin, fins or tail are often caused by parasites or bacterial infections, which need medication. Some skin problems ay not be visible in themselves but are indicated by the h's obvious discomfort, with frequent scratching and pid breathing. Others can be seen as growths, blotches, mps or white specks, thread-like parasites trailing from e body, a velvety coating to the skin, or shredded fins. sk your local specialist shop for suitable medication.

## 46 Swimbladder problems

Fish which lose their balance and helplessly float, sink or even swim upside down have swimbladder disease (see page 10). Causes include poor water quality, digestive problems, parasites or simply keeping more vulnerable fancy goldfish varieties. Swimbladder disorders are often incurable. However, improving water quality and reducing food may help, as may a saltwater bath one dessert spoon of salt per 4.5litre/1gal of water). Don't use table salt with dded iodine: you can buy special aquarium salt, which is safer.

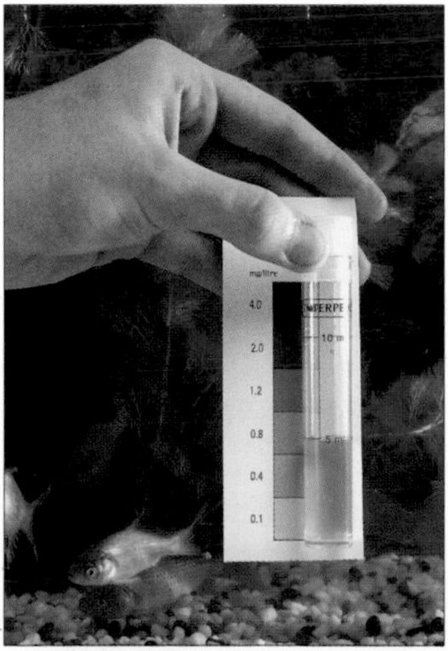


*Right: Test kits are available to heck levels of ammonia, nitrites and nitrates in the water. These are by-products of fish waste which build up in an aquarium and can be harmful to the fish.*

## GOLD MEDAL TIPS

### SEEK ADVICE

*If you have any cause for concern, don't delay in seeking advice. Good petshops and aquatic dealers are happy to help and will stock a range of suitable treatments. Give them as much information as you can so that they can assess the situation accurately. Bringing along a sample of tank water may help them to diagnose the problem.*

### ITCHY ICH

*One of the commonest parasitic infections is whitespot disease, or ich. Early signs are scratching and discomfort, but later the parasites are visible as tiny white spots, like grains of salt. You will need to medicate the tank immediately with a proprietary whitespot cure for at least ten days, following the instructions carefully.*

### FINS AND TAILS

*Injured fins and tails can often repair themselves. However, a whitish edging to fin damage means the start of fin rot, caused by bacterial infection. Never neglect this sign. If left untreated, it will destroy the fins and move on to attack body tissue.*

# GOLD MEDAL TIPS

**BREEDING CONDITIONS**

*To encourage breeding, create an artificial summertime in their tank by increasing the hours of lighting, carrying out daily 20 per cent water changes, and adding live or frozen food, such as brine shrimp, to the diet.*

**MOPPING UP**

*Professional breeders make the transfer of eggs to a nursery tank easier by providing spawning mops for the eggs to stick to. You can make a mop by tying lengths of wool into a tassel and fixing this to a cork to float in the aquarium.*

*Below: Breeding tubercles appear behind the male's eyes.*

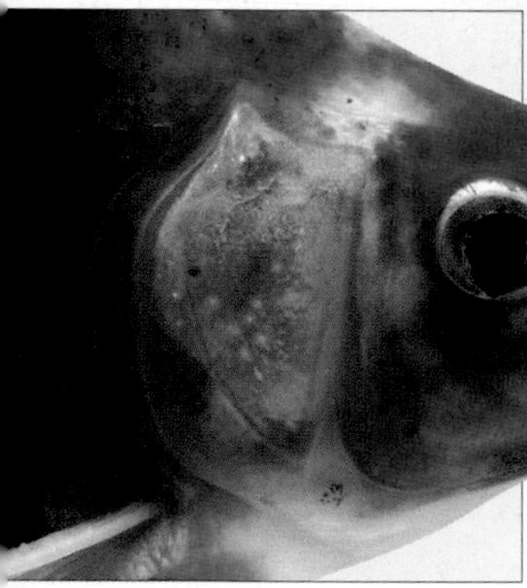

**MIX AND MATCH**

*All goldfish varieties can breed with each other, so if different types are kept together they may produce some interesting (or disappointing) crossbreeds. In ponds, goldfish will also interbreed with koi and ghost carp, producing babies with characteristics of both species.*

47

## Not for beginners

Breeding goldfish is not a task for the novice fishkeeper. Not only do you need space for a nursery tank to raise the babies (and a home for any youngsters that survive), but eggs and hatchlings require a lot of care. Eggs are vulnerable to fungus growths, and newly hatched goldfish, at only 5mm (0.2in) long, are extremely fragile. They need good, stable water conditions and temperatures and correct quantities of special food if they are to survive.

*Above: Nine-week-old red metallic ranchus already have a good shape, but their hoods may take three years to develop.*

48

## The goldfish breeding cycle

Goldfish don't breed until mature (usually in their second year). In the breeding season females grow plumper, and males develop round white spots (breeding tubercles) on their heads, gill covers and pectoral fins. Goldfish courtship consists of males chasing females for several days before spawning (egg-laying) occurs. Once the eggs are laid, there is no parental care, and indeed goldfish regularly eat their young.

# BREEDING TIPS

49

## Goldfish are unlikely to breed in ordinary aquarium conditions

Breeding is more likely in large outdoor ponds. It is impossible to sex goldfish outside the breeding season, so you may not even have a pair. If your fish start to indulge in mad chasing sessions, they are probably in breeding condition and may lay pinhead-sized eggs, which stick to plant leaves and hatch out four to six days later. Unless you can transfer these to a nursery aquarium, your breeding programme ends here, as the adults quickly devour hatchlings.

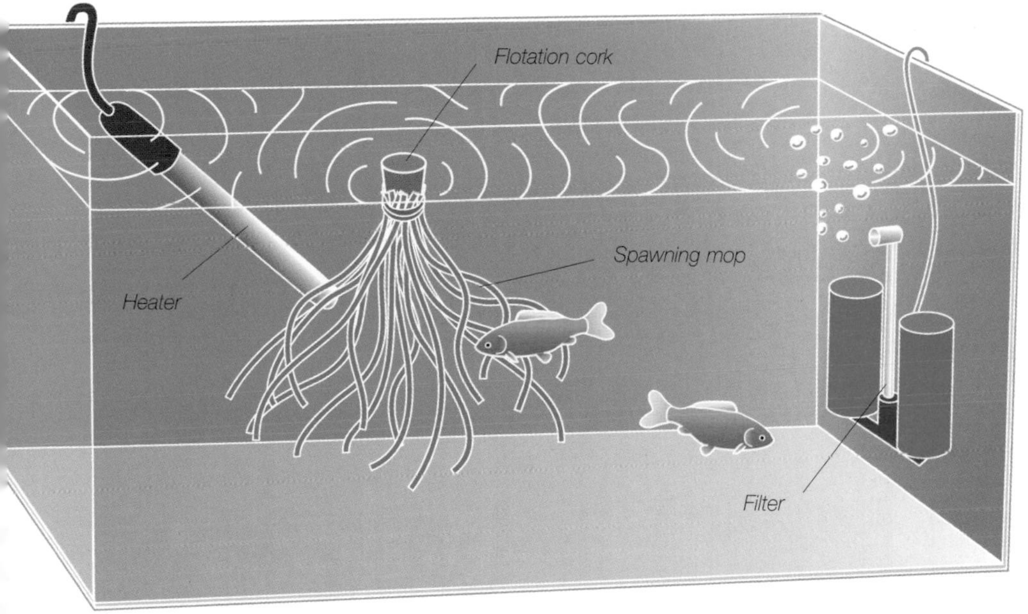


*Above: Serious breeders use a large, heated breeding tank with a spawning mop to which the eggs can stick.*

50

## Care of eggs and young

If you have a spare aquarium and want to try raising young, remove egg-covered plants to this nursery, where they require temperature of about 21°C (70°F). Newly-hatched young (fry) look like tiny hairs tached to the plants at first. For the first few days they don't need feeding, as they are ill absorbing food from their yolk sacs. When they swim away from the plants, they need ɔecial fry food consisting of microscopic organisms and algae.

# Further Information

## Recommended Books

Andrews, Dr Chris, *Guide to Fancy Goldfish* (Interpet Publishing, 1996)
Brewster, Bernice, *An Essential Guide to Keeping Goldfish* (Interpet Publishing, 2003)
Ostrow, Marshall, *Goldfish – A Complete Pet Owner's Manual* (Barron's, 1995)
Page, Gill, *Getting To Know Your Goldfish* (Interpet Publishing, 2001)
Sands, Dr David, *Caring For Your Pet Goldfish* (Interpet Publishing, 1996)
Windsor, Steve, *Pet Owner's Guide to the Goldfish* (Ringpress Books, 1996)

## Clubs

The Goldfish Society of America, P.O. Box 551373, Fort Lauderdale, FL 33555, USA
The Goldfish Society of Great Britain, 62 Balstonia Drive, Stanford le Hope, Essex, SS17 8HX, UK.

## Recommended Websites

http://www.goldfishinfo.com
http://www.petlibrary.com/goldfish/goldfish.html
http://kokosgoldfish.com
http://animalsoup.net/aquaria/index.html

### Acknowledgements

The author and publisher would like to offer sincere thanks to Jackie Wilson of Rolf C. Hagen (UK) Ltd and Sarah Chapman of Reef One Ltd who generously supplied equipment for photography in this book. Thanks also go to models Alexia McGuire and Victoria and Louise Etheridge, to Mike and Wendy Yendell at Aristaquatics, Billingshurst, and to Peter Dean at Interpet Ltd for his help with photographic props.

### Picture Credits

The majority of the photographs reproduced were taken by Neil Sutherland specifically for this book and are the copyright of Interpet Publishing. Geoffrey Rogers of Ideas Into Print also kindly supplied a number of photographs (© Interpet Publishing) – many thanks to him for his assistance.